UN PLUG GED

UN PLUG GED

PRAYER
the Powerful Wireless Connection

DWIGHT SHAWROD RIDDICK II
KELLI SWEAT   KISHA MCDANIEL   JENNELL RIDDICK

Suffolk, Virginia

UNPLUGGED:
PRAYER the Powerful Wirelesss Connection

Copyright © 2020 by Dwight Shawrod Riddick II, Kelli Sweat, Kisha McDaniel, and Jennell Riddick
All rights reserved.

All rights reserved. This book is protected by the copyright laws of the United States of America. This book may not be copied or reprinted for commercial gain or profit. The use of quotations or occasional page copying for personal or group study is permitted and encouraged. Permission will be granted upon request.

Final Step Publishing, LLC

PO Box 1441
Suffolk, VA 23439

Soft cover ISBN: 978-1-7349784-9-0
E-book - ISBN: 978-1-7355280-0-7

For Worldwide Distribution. Printed in U.S.A.

DEDICATION

To Bishop Curtis and Lady Evelyn Edmonds who served the St. Mark Missionary Baptist Church from 1992 - 2018. We are all blessed by your vision for a prayer room, prayer time, and building God's place of worship on a foundation of bibles at 2714 Frederick Blvd. To you we dedicate this book.

ACKNOWLEDGMENTS

During the most difficult times in the life of the church, God has always had special people that He assigns to special tasks of prayer. I want to thank those whom God has called for such a time as this.

To Bishop and Lady Edmonds, thank you for being spiritually mindful enough to identify an intentional space for worshippers to pray. The third floor of St. Mark has a special place in the hearts of many, including God. I also want to thank Dave and Janis Starkey for their dedication to caring for the St. Mark Prayer room. They are constantly keeping the plants watered, the area clean, and the upper room prepared for prayer. This dedication brings life not just to the space, but brings life to the atmosphere of prayer for our entire ministry.

I appreciate Dr. Valarie Hall who is a devoted prayer warrior with over 25 years of training in intercessory prayer. She leads the Hampton Roads' Intercessory Prayer Network, yet found time to submit a powerful prayer over this resource and provide the foreword to kick off this prayer log. I'd like to thank Kelli Sweat, a Master of Divinity student at the Samuel DeWitt Procter of School of Theology, and Minister Kisha McDaniel, who is the founder of Purpose Pursuit Ministries. They were both eager, beyond their administrative duties at St. Mark, to offer heart felt daily prayer submissions.

To Dr. Jennell Riddick, who has led the St. Mark prayer ministry weekly in connecting with God, and covers the sanctuary and church consistently with intercession. Thank you for your intro and opening prayer.

St. Mark family, community friends, and those who are Kingdom connected, thank you for supporting this resource and committing to the 100,000 hours of prayer challenge. Together we are going to change the world.

Lastly, but not least, I honor the Spirit of God, Jesus Christ, and God our Father for hearing these prayers and blessing each person who will use this resource to enhance their prayer life.

FOREWORD

Buzz. Beep. Static. In today's technology driven society, most people are too familiar with these energy draining sounds. This should not be the case for Christians. Believers should hear the still, small voice of God louder than anything else. Drs. Dwight and Jennell Riddick understand this concept. In their book, *Unplugged: Prayer The Powerful Wireless Connection,* readers will explore ways to disconnect from others' voices to fellowship with God.

As an intercessor for more than twenty-five years, I know prayer works. The principles presented in this book are the ones Jesus used to turn the world upside down. Every time the noise of life intensified, Jesus unplugged. He intentionally spent time in prayer with the Father to receive instruction and life-sustaining power to defeat the enemy. Now, it is your time to do the same.

Over the next thirty-one days and beyond, I invite you to be intentional about using these proven strategies to talk to and hear from God. As you embark on this journey with your Father, be deliberate. Recognize He hears you and will respond. Expect and record His supernatural response.

Unplug from the world, disconnect from distractions, and power up in God!

Dr. Valerie Hall
Intercessory Ministry Leader
Perfecting Saints Church and Intercessors' Network of Hampton Roads

PREFACE

My family was sitting at the dinner table enjoying a great evening of catching up and my wife's favorite seafood dish. We often play this game my son created that we call "Categories." It's an easy game. Someone chooses a category and we go around the table naming things that are within that category. As long as you don't repeat what anyone else has said or fail to provide an answer, you are in the game. While playing, my son chooses the category of sea creatures.

My 6-year- old daughter screams out "smalltooth fish!" We all burst into laughter because none of us had ever heard of that before. This has to be her childlike imagination running wild again, right? Yet, she persisted in telling us, "No, it's a real thing. I saw it on YouTube." We, of course being older than her, attempted to let her down gently, helping her to understand that there's no such thing. She insists that there is a sea creature known as the smalltooth fish and screams out, "Hey Google, what is a smalltooth fish!" The little grey device resting on a counter across the room lights up and begins explaining that a smalltooth fish is a rare sawfish found in shallow tropical water. I exclaim, "What?! Who knew that?"

My wife is laughing hysterically and my son answers what was supposed to be a rhetorical question, "Google! Dad, Google knows everything." I looked at him, eyebrows arched, and slightly disturbed and said, "You mean God, right?" He responds, "Of course God knows everything, but Google knows too." Then they all burst into gut-busting laughter. Being the dad, I had to have the last word, so I say, "I bet you Google wouldn't know anything if I unplugged him." My son's eyes widened as if he were a deer in headlights. "Dad, what do you mean unplug Google? Why would you unplug him?" I responded, "First of all we are not going to keep talking about Google like's it's a real person." Then I laughed. "Secondly, what would y'all do if I unplugged Google? Who would you talk to about smalltooth fish then?" We all laughed, congratulated Jasmine on her genius answer, and picked a new category.

That family moment may not sound significant, but I think it provides some spiritual insights. The role Google played that night is the role God wants to have every day. Sure, Google confirmed her answer about the smalltooth fish, but getting unplugged from the Googles of life allow us to get truly connected to God who created the smalltooth fish. God wants us to have questions and seek and desire conversation with Him. He wants us to scream across the room to Him, "Hey God, what's a smallmouth fish?" Then like Google sitting over on a counter across the room, God will light up and in return will enlighten us. Of course, He may or may not tell you descriptive details about a smalltooth fish when you ask. However, he knows. He knows the answer to that and every other question you have. He has strategies for your success, plans for you to prosper, words to correct our misdeeds, and at a bare minimum, He simply wants to talk to you as a good father does wanting to be in relationship with his child. So, consider getting Unplugged.

To be clear, I am not saying A.I. is bad nor am I saying we should turn off all of our smart devices. Both of my children were born as natives to all of this new A.I. technology. My wife and I are more like immigrants to this land ruled by Alexa, Siri, Google, Bixby, and other info distributing digital

A.I. We grew up on read it yourself Encyclopedia Britannica. Our daughter Jasmine relied on YouTube and son Dwight relied on Google. They are like many of us today using Artificial Intelligence to access information, find answers, and unearth new revelations. While I absolutely have no fight with technology, I would remind you that there is a benefit in getting unplugged.

Pulling the cord, disconnecting from the wall, and turning off the lights. That's the image that we would like to present. There should be some time regularly that we all disconnect from the restraining walls of worry in the world. We should pull the tangling cord on all of the cares and concerns of the communities we are in. We should turn the blinding, blinking lights off and avoid the bright glare that causes us to perform for others in order to be accepted. We must all learn that while there is some information to gain from AI, there is so much more of our lives lost until we get unplugged.

Getting unplugged is the simple idea of relying less on artificial intelligence and getting real revelation from God. Getting unplugged is deciding that while there are many voices in the world, you will prioritize God above all. Getting unplugged is the act of setting aside intentional time to spend with God and not only conversing with Him for emergencies or by accident. This resource is provided as our attempt to get you down on your knees and reaching towards familiar outlets to unplug from your vices of comfort and tapping into a true wireless network of life transforming prayer. This resource is a guide to help you GET UNPLUGGED.

Dr. Dwight Shawrod Riddick, II
Senior Pastor St. Mark Church

Introduction

Contents

Introduction	11
How to Use this Book	13

Part 1
LOG YOUR PRAYER
    Prayer Log — 16

Part 2
LEARNING PRAYER
    ACTS Prayer Model — 26
    Create Your Own ACTS — 30

Part 3
LIVING THROUGH PRAYER
    Opening Prayer by Dr. Jennell — 32
    31 Days of ACTS Prayer — 33

Part 4
LISTENING IN PRAYER
    4 Ways to Hear God Clearer — 66
    Additional Prayer Resources — 71

Part 5
LEARNING PRAYER - Appendix
    Types of Prayers — 74
    In Jesus' Name — 88
    Why Say Amen — 91
    Closing Prayer by Dr. D.S. Riddick — 94

Introduction

Why do we pray? Why do we use models of prayer? Why are we logging prayers?

We pray because there are simply some things that never go out of style! Times change, people change, but isn't it good to know that our God remains the same! We pray because the prayers of the righteous availeth much. We pray because it is a command. We pray because we want to connect with the Lord. We pray because we believe that prayers changes things, and prayer changes us.

While God remains a consistent presence and source of protection and provision in our lives, the promise and power of prayer remains accessible to each of us. Tap into the ultimate power source. It doesn't make sense to live depleted, deficient, or defeated when you have an open invitation to get plugged in! So, as you use this book as a tool, be reminded of the limitless power of God that can meet you right where you are! Take intentional time to consistently unplug from the world and its distractions in order to tap into godly power, wisdom, and direction. Prayer works! Let it work for you and bless you!

In this book we are using the ACTS model of prayer. It is a useful tool to help us center our minds and offer our petitions and thanksgiving to God. It helps us to recognize the importance of having a balanced prayer life that includes praise, confession, thanksgiving, supplication, and listening to God. Finally, we are logging time in prayer so that we are intentional about setting aside this time with God. He is waiting to hear you pray. Yes, you! You are important to Him. We also look forward to seeing the cumulative number of hours that we invest as the larger body of Christ. Thank you for accepting this kingdom commitment to pray! We are expecting great things! We indeed are better together!

Dr. Jennell Riddick
Executive Minister of St. Mark Church

How to Use this Book

It has been said that you cannot manage what you do not measure. One goal of our relationship with Christ should be to increase or enhance our prayer lives. This resource has been provided to assist in both. We suggest that you:

Log
Write down the amount of times or what times you pray as well as when and how God answers those prayers.

Learn
We highly recommend implementing the ACTS prayer model. In the appendix, there are six models. I encourage you to use this resource to learn alternate connecting ways before beginning your daily prayers.

Listen
After reading the prayer and writing the prayer, you should take a moment to sit still and listen. There should be no talking, worshipping, or using any gadgets. Simply be still and listen to what God has to say.

Live
Read the short daily ACTS structured prayers then respond to them in the journal or write your own prayers. The reading and writing connect you to God in a personal way. Expect God to answer your prayers. Since you are expecting it, you should keep your eyes and spirit open to seeing what God is doing, then chronicle His response. You will begin the devotionals being led by an opening prayer by Dr. Jennell Riddick.

Learn Appendix
We provide multiple prayer models for you to choose and pattern. While we highly recommend implementing the ACTS prayer model, you can use this resource to learn alternate connecting ways.

Closing Prayer by Pastor Riddick
This book ends with a covering and closing prayer by our Pastor. We hope that serves as a reminder that you are not in this walk of life alone. You are covered in prayer, you have a partner in pursuing God's promise, and you have an intercessor seeking God with and for you often.

LOG YOUR PRAYER

Then the LORD replied: "Write down the revelation and make it plain on tablets so that a herald may run with it.
Habakkuk 2:2

PRAYER LOG

What to do?
If possible, identify a time and space each day that you will meet God for prayer. Whether it's two minutes, twenty minutes, two hours, or anywhere in between, the goal is to have a standing appointment to commune with Him. You can pray anywhere and anytime or everywhere and all of the time. So, do not overthink your prayer life. We are simply providing a systematic way for you to measure your growth in the practice of praying.

Write it down.
After you have prayed, come back and chart your progress. You may track it in any way that is most comfortable for you. You do not have to chart each method. We have provided various methods for you to track your progress with a daily, weekly, or monthly log chart.

You will be able to use the log to:

- Keep you accountable
- Track your progress
- Identify your personal prayer time trends
- See what days may be more challenging than others
- Most of all, account for the amount of time you intentionally spend with God.

WEEKLY PRAYER LOG

This is the most common way we encourage you to log your prayer time. At the end of each day, simply reflect and write down a good approximation of the number of minutes or hours that you spent praying. At the end of the week, tally up your responses and assess your progress.

Week	Sun	Mon	Tues	Wed	Thurs	Fri	Sat	Total Hours Prayed
Example 8/5/2020	20min	10min	5min	40min	15min	8min	1 hour	
					Total Time for Month =			

DAILY PRAYER LOG

You may use this to log when you pray each day. It is not mandatory. This is provided for your convenience and as a reminder that God is looking for you to set an appointment with Him. This schedule will allow you to see the times that you most frequently meet God for intimate conversation.

Time	SUN	MON	TUES	WED	THURS	FRI	SAT
12:00 a.m.							
1:00 a.m.							
2:00 a.m.							
3:00 a.m.							
4:00 a.m.							
5:00 a.m.							
6:00 a.m.							
7:00 a.m.							
8:00 a.m.							
9:00 a.m.							
10:00 a.m.							
11:00 a.m.							
12:00 Noon							
1:00 p.m.							
2:00 p.m.							

_____Log Your Prayer

Time	SUN	MON	TUES	WED	THURS	FRI	SAT
3:00 p.m.							
4:00 p.m.							
5:00 p.m.							
6:00 p.m.							
7:00 p.m.							
8:00 p.m.							
9:00 p.m.							
10:00 p.m.							
11:00 p.m.							

MONTHLY PRAYER LOG

Write in under each month the amount of time you have logged praying. Transfer these totals from your Weekly Log.

Jan.	Feb.	Mar.	Apr.	May	June
July	Aug.	Sept.	Oct.	Nov.	Dec.
		Annual Total Prayer Time =			

UNPLUGGED

Prayer Requests

_____ Log Your Prayer

What I Am Praying For

Family/Friends	Local Community	World
Church	Sick	Myself

How God Answers These Prayers

How God Answers These Prayers

Family/Friends	Local Community	World

Church	Sick	Myself

LEARNING PRAYER

One day Jesus was praying in a certain place. When he finished, one of his disciples said to him, "Lord, teach us to pray, just as John taught his disciples."
Luke 11:1

LET'S PRAY

Summary of ACTS Model of Prayer

I do not know if there is a right or wrong way to pray, but I do believe that there are some great models for prayer. Included in the appendix are six models for prayer that can guide you in being clear about your prayer time. We highly recommend the ACTS model as one to use often. I would remind you that even on your best day with the most eloquent words, we must always still depend on the Holy Spirit to guide our prayer time. Paul writes in Romans 8:26, "In the same way, the Spirit helps us in our weakness. We do not know what we ought to pray for, but the Spirit himself intercedes for us through wordless groans." Here is the ACTS prayer model, but I would encourage you to jump to the appendix before beginning your daily prayers for additional references to various ways to connect through prayer.

A - Adoration

C - Confession

T - Thanksgiving

S - Supplication

Adoration
Worship, something about God and use a name of God.

Confession
State something you believe or acknowledge a sin.

Thanksgiving
State something you praise God for doing or acting in your life.

Supplication
Ask God for something or make a request.

Adoration – The *A* in the ACTS model stands for adoration, which means to adore, worship, glorify, and exalt God. The goal is to say something to God about God. This is usually where you state God's name or a superlative or descriptive name of God. For Example: "You are Jehovah, or You have been my healer." The goal is to in intimate ways adore or show adoration towards God.

Through adoration, we show our loyalty and admiration of God. This is when we worship God simply for who He is without asking for anything. It is legitimately just acknowledging that you know who He is. This could be a song of praise to Him, praying a psalm of worship, declaring His attributes, or a myriad of other forms of worship.

Confession – The *C* in the ACTS model stands for confession. The word *confess* means "to agree with." The key to confession is understanding that it could be a confession of one of two things. You can speak confessions of sins or transgressions against God, or you can you simply make confessions about things that you believe are truths.

When we confess our sins, we agree with God that we are wrong and that we have sinned against Him by what we have said, thought, or done. God forgives us and restores our fellowship with Him (1 John 1:9). Confessing sins is not the lowering of yourself, but it is really the lifting of Jesus. The goal is not to degrade yourself but to acknowledge a need for Jesus; therefore, confessing sins is a sort of celebration.

Confessing is also making statements that declare what you believe. To say, "God, it has been you guiding me through life's storms and sheltering me from life's rains" is a confession. It says, I believe this is true. In the ACTS model, try to balance out your prayer with some confession of sin and some confessions of facts.

<u>Thanksgiving</u> – The *T* represents thanksgiving. Philippians 4:6 says, "With thanksgiving let your requests be made known to God" (ESV). This is when we simply say thank you. It is probably the most common form of prayer. You can say thank you or use alternate words like, "I am grateful, I appreciate, I honor you for doing _____." It is acknowledging what God has done and how He has acted upon your life.

While it may sound similar to adoration, there are some differences. Adoration focuses on who God is; thanksgiving focuses on what God has done. We can thank God for many things including His love, salvation, protection, and provision. We encourage you to be as specific as possible in this stage of prayer. In place of, "God thank you for blessing me or protecting me," you should consider saying, "God thank you for providing so that I could pay my utility bill, or thank you for causing others to stop at red lights and not T-bone me at an intersection." Be as specific as possible. The old church used to sing a song with lyrics that said, "Count your blessings and name them one by one." That is our recommendation during this step of prayer.

<u>Supplication</u> – The *S* stands for supplication, which refers to prayer for our and others' needs. One way to remember what supplication entails is to think of its root word *supply*. This is the step in prayer where you ask God to provide or supply. This is where you make your request known to God or make a petition. Your request can be tangible, spiritual, emotional, and most of all, for someone other than yourself. Paul encouraged us to make "supplication for all the saints" (Ephesians 6:18, ESV), which means to pray diligently for our brothers and sisters in Christ.

Create your own ACTS Prayer

What words of affirmation and adoration could you use?

_____

_____

_____

What confessions could you make?

_____

_____

_____

Is there anything you could thank God for?

_____

_____

_____

What would you ask God for if you could have anything right now?

_____

_____

_____

LIVING THROUGH PRAYER

But Jesus often withdrew to lonely places and prayed.
Luke 5:16

Write therefore the things that you have seen, those that are and those that are to take place after this.
Revelation 1:19

Opening Prayer by Dr. Jennell Riddick

Heavenly Father, we honor and bless you today for who you are and all that you continue to do in our lives. We acknowledge that it is in you that we live, move, and have our being. As we come today, we thank you that there is nothing too hard for you. We thank you that you are concerned about every part of who we are: mentally, emotionally, spiritually, and physically.

Please continue to grow us in faith and wisdom. Please cleanse our hearts, renew our minds, and continue to draw us closer to you. May you be pleased with all that we say and do.

We submit our plans and desires to you, trusting that you have plans to prosper us and not harm us, to give us hope and a future. We will continue to trust in you and your unfailing love towards us.

Even in times of uncertainty and difficulty, our faith and trust will be in you because you promised that you would never leave nor forsake us. You tell us in your word that you are a present help in our time of need.

Thank you for shining your darkness piercing light in us and through us. Thank you for the blessings that are yet to come. Our expectation is in you.

In Jesus' Name,

Amen.

DAY 1

God, you are a wise and all-knowing Master.
I do not understand all that is taking place in our country,
Yet I am thankful for your continued protection each day.
Please grant me discernment so that I will make decisions that please you.
In Jesus' Name, Amen.

What do you sense (feel, hear, envision)?

_____

_____

_____

_____

_____

_____

_____

_____

_____

_____

DAY 2

Lord, you are my balm in Gilead and a healer of the heart.
I have had those I love abuse my kindness and I am broken.
In my pain, I am grateful that you never left me. I praise you for your faithfulness.
Continue to remind me that you never leave me and let me experience the joy of your presence.
In Jesus' Name, Amen.

What do you sense (feel, hear, envision)?

_____
_____
_____
_____
_____
_____
_____
_____
_____
_____

DAY 3

You are my Father in heaven that has made your presence felt on earth.
Today, I repent because I have anger that often overtakes me.
I praise you because your anger only lasts for a moment, but your favor lasts a lifetime.
God, give me peace so that I, too, will experience heaven on earth.
In Jesus' Name, Amen.

What do you sense (feel, hear, envision)?

_____

_____

_____

_____

_____

_____

_____

_____

_____

DAY 4

God, you are Elohim, far above any other God.
I often put my trust in earthly systems.
I am grateful that you still love me anyway.
Please give me the wisdom to distinguish the God opportunities from the good opportunities.
In Jesus' Name, Amen.

What do you sense (feel, hear, envision)?

_____
_____
_____
_____
_____
_____
_____
_____
_____
_____

DAY 5

God, you have been my way maker.
I sometimes doubt that the promises you made to me will happen.
Thank you for the small and the grand ways that you show me that you see me and care for me.
Grant me the patience, peace, and perseverance to follow your will for me and to live a blessed life.
In Jesus' Name, Amen.

What do you sense (feel, hear, envision)?

_____
_____
_____
_____
_____
_____
_____
_____

DAY 6

God, as the earth revolves around the Sun, my life revolves around you. You are my central source.
There are times when I want to be a know it all.
Thank you for your patience with me and for growing my capacity.
Grant me insight to know when to speak and when to be quiet in order to be the best resource to others.
In Jesus' Name, Amen.

What do you sense (feel, hear, envision)?

___
___
___
___
___
___
___
___

DAY 7

Abba, Father.
Sometimes I feel far away from you.
Thank you for loving me like no one else can. Thank you for holding me in your hand.
Allow me to feel your love and presence today.
In Jesus' Name, Amen.

What do you sense (feel, hear, envision)?

_____

_____

_____

_____

_____

_____

_____

_____

_____

_____

DAY 8

Lord, you are Elohim. You are the creator and sustainer of all things.
I feel stuck where I am. I am weak.
I know that in my weakness you have perfect strength.
God restore unto me my zeal and determination.
In Jesus' Name, Amen.

What do you sense (feel, hear, envision)?

_____
_____
_____
_____
_____
_____
_____
_____
_____
_____
_____

DAY 9

Almighty God, you are awesome in all your ways.
There are times when I take for granted the things you have done for me.
Thank you for blessing me despite me.
Allow me to daily remember all the great things you have done for me.
In Jesus' Name, Amen.

What do you sense (feel, hear, envision)?

_____

_____

_____

_____

_____

_____

_____

_____

_____

DAY 10

God, you are Shalom, my peace.
There are times when I get caught up in the hustle and bustle of life and become overwhelmed.
Even when life tries to weigh me down you are an ever-present help.
Give me discernment to plan my day according to your direction and the grace to execute your plan.
In Jesus' Name, Amen.

What do you sense (feel, hear, envision)?

_____
_____
_____
_____
_____
_____
_____
_____
_____

DAY 11

Jehovah Rapha, my healer.
With all that is going on in life sometimes I neglect myself.
You protect my mind, body, and soul day and night.
Allow me to be more disciplined in taking care of the temple you have given my so that every part of my being will prosper.
In Jesus' Name, Amen.

What do you sense (feel, hear, envision)?

DAY 12

My God, you are my sanctifier.
There are times when I struggle with standing up for what is right when faced with adversity.
You always ensure victory to those who called according to your purpose.
Grant me the boldness of Deborah, Jael, Rahab, and Esther.
In Jesus' Name, Amen.

What do you sense (feel, hear, envision)?

_____
_____
_____
_____
_____
_____
_____
_____
_____
_____

DAY 13

God, you are the master gardener.
Sometimes I forget that I am an extension of Jesus, the true vine.
Thank you for pruning me, providing for me, and helping me grow.
Continue to shine on me so that I may be an example of what your love looks like to others.
In Jesus' Name, Amen.

What do you sense (feel, hear, envision)?

_____

_____

_____

_____

_____

_____

_____

_____

_____

_____

DAY 14

God, you are the lifter of my head.
There are times when I feel low and unworthy.
Thank you for reminding me that I am fearfully and wonderfully made.
Continue to give me the godly confidence that empowers me.
In Jesus' Name, Amen.

What do you sense (feel, hear, envision)?

_____
_____
_____
_____
_____
_____
_____
_____
_____
_____
_____

DAY 15

God, you are mighty in battle.
Sometimes I feel defeated and I want to throw in the towel.
Thank you for reminding me that when I put on the full armor of God, I have the victory.
Continue to remind me of your sacred word that remains true forever.
In Jesus' Name, Amen.

What do you sense (feel, hear, envision)?

_____
_____
_____
_____
_____
_____
_____
_____
_____
_____

DAY 16

Lord, you are my joy.
Lately, the media and news reports have been overwhelming.
Thank you for revealing to me that there is joy and peace in you.
Bring to my remembrance the fruits of the spirit: love, joy, peace, kindness, faithfulness, and patience.
In Jesus' Name, Amen.

What do you sense (feel, hear, envision)?

_____

_____

_____

_____

_____

_____

_____

_____

_____

_____

DAY 17

God, you are a way maker.
Sometimes I don't see how things will work out.
Thank you for giving us an expected end, a hope, and a future.
Remind me that even when I am unsure, you do all things well.
In Jesus' Name, Amen.

What do you sense (feel, hear, envision)?

_____

_____

_____

_____

_____

_____

_____

_____

_____

_____

DAY 18

Dear God, you are Jehovah Rohi, The Lord our Shepherd.
I am aware that evil is always present.
Thank you for your protection from dangers seen and unseen.
Give me the wisdom to remain in your will and protection.
In Jesus' Name, Amen.

What do you sense (feel, hear, envision)?

_____
_____
_____
_____
_____
_____
_____
_____
_____
_____

DAY 19

God, your love is perfect and has no boundaries.
Today, I repent for allowing my judgment and criticism of others to block me from being a true friend.
I am grateful that your loving kindness is ever working to draw each of us closer to you.
Father, I ask that you fill my heart with compassion and empathy so that I may share your character and message with those you love.
In Jesus' Name, Amen.

What do you sense (feel, hear, envision)?

_____

_____

_____

_____

_____

_____

_____

_____

DAY 20

Father, you are omnipresent; you are EVERYWHERE!
This season of social distancing has caused me to feel isolated, lonely, and alone.
Yet, I take comfort in your promise to never leave or forsake me. Thank you for your constant presence.
Help me to experience your loving arms of protection, comfort, and peace reminding me that wherever I am, you are always with me.
In Jesus' Name, Amen.

What do you sense (feel, hear, envision)?

_____
_____
_____
_____
_____
_____
_____
_____

DAY 21

Creator of heaven and earth, you are a perfect and loving Father.
Lately, I have been short tempered and impatient with loved ones.
Though I may fail you, I'm grateful that you still call me your child.
Lord, check my heart and fill me with your spirit of love, joy, peace, patience, kindness, gentleness, and self-control.
In Jesus' Name, Amen.

What do you sense (feel, hear, envision)?

_____
_____
_____
_____
_____
_____
_____
_____

DAY 22

Dear God, you are a faithful and loving Father.
Lately, I have allowed fear and anxiety to impact my daily life.
Yet, I am grateful for your perfect love that casts out fear and provides hope.
Please help me navigate through each day with your power, love, and sound mind.
In Jesus' Name, Amen.

What do you sense (feel, hear, envision)?

_____

_____

_____

_____

_____

_____

_____

_____

_____

DAY 23

Mighty God, you are my banner and source of protection.
I'm worried that the brutality and violence of this world will impact my family.
I know that our life is in your hands and I praise you for being a loving Father who watches over us day and night.
Father, cover my family in the blood of Jesus and surround them with your angels' protection. Let no trouble fall on them and no evil influence their hearts.
In Jesus' Name, Amen.

What do you sense (feel, hear, envision)?

_____
_____
_____
_____
_____
_____
_____
_____
_____

DAY 24

God, you are sovereign, and all things are under your authority.
Today, I repent for worrying about money.
Thank you for supplying my needs and granting me favor and divine strategies for financial increase.
Father, forgive me for not trusting you and help me to submit all things, including my money, under your authority so that I may experience your joy.
In Jesus' Name, Amen.

What do you sense (feel, hear, envision)?

_____
_____
_____
_____
_____
_____
_____
_____
_____

DAY 25

God, you are magnificent, an all-knowing and all-wise Father.

I have not achieved the goals I set for myself and I feel defeated.

Only you know why I was created. Thank you for your gentle nudges and peaceful whispers that draw me closer to you and my life's purpose.

Lord, help me to release the grip on my life, transfer my control over to you, and allow you to direct my path for your glory.

In Jesus' Name, Amen.

What do you sense (feel, hear, envision)?

_____

_____

_____

_____

_____

_____

_____

_____

DAY 26

God, you are a just and loving Father.
Between gossip and harsh words, sometimes I can't believe the things that I say.
Thank you for your loving grace and mercy that extends forgiveness, correction, and restoration.
Father, guard my tongue so that I no longer commit to unwholesome talk but only what is helpful to building up others so that you will be pleased with me.
In Jesus' Name, Amen.

What do you sense (feel, hear, envision)?

_____
_____
_____
_____
_____
_____
_____
_____
_____

DAY 27

Lord, you are my King and the lover of my soul.
I repent today for allowing my desire for physical companionship to interrupt my quality time with you.
Great is your love for me! I am grateful for your patience and daily reminders that you are always with me.
Teach me how to choose you daily and walk by your word so that each step will lead me closer to you.
In Jesus' Name, Amen.

What do you sense (feel, hear, envision)?

_____

_____

_____

_____

_____

_____

_____

_____

_____

DAY 28

Eternal God, you are my provider.
I regret that I have put my trust and confidence in external resources when you alone are my source.
Thank you for the blessings you have given me and my family out of your many riches.
Help us to use those blessings to be a blessing and resource to others.
In Jesus' Name, Amen.

What do you sense (feel, hear, envision)?

_____
_____
_____
_____
_____
_____
_____
_____
_____

DAY 29

Gracious heavenly Father, you are Jehovah Rapha – The Lord my Healer.
It is in times of sickness and pain where I feel feeble, restless, impatient, and useless.
Thank you for your mercy and sufficient grace that is made perfect in times of weakness.
Father, may your healing hand rest upon me with life-giving power for restoration, wholeness, and renewed strength so that I may continue in your service.
In Jesus' Name, Amen.

What do you sense (feel, hear, envision)?

_____
_____
_____
_____
_____
_____
_____
_____

DAY 30

Father, you are a just and righteous God.
I confess that I have committed sin against you and the shame of my actions are haunting me.
Though I have wronged you, I thank you for your saving grace and the gift of freedom through Jesus Christ.
Lord, please shine the light of your Holy Spirit into the dark places of my heart, expose my sin, and reconcile me back to you so that my life brings glory to your name.
In Jesus' Name, Amen.

What do you sense (feel, hear, envision)?

_____

_____

_____

_____

_____

_____

_____

_____

DAY 31

Magnificent Father God, you are the King of Glory!
There is no person on earth that deserves more praise and honor than you.
Thank you for loving me and watching over me. I will praise you as long as I live.
Amazing Father, please forgive me for my shortcomings and allow your ears to be attentive to my prayers. Great and marvelous are your works! You alone are holy and worthy of all worship. May your name be praised!
In Jesus' Name, Amen.

What do you sense (feel, hear, envision)?

_____
_____
_____
_____
_____
_____
_____

LISTENING IN PRAYER

When the Spirit of truth comes, he will guide you into all the truth, for he will not speak on his own authority, but whatever he hears he will speak, and he will declare to you the things that are to come.
John 16:13

LISTEN

Prayer has often been associated with people talking with God. While that is true, it is not the complete truth. Prayer is communication between God and humanity. The difference is that the former only gives us permission to speak. The latter gives way for us to listen and hear from God. Listening in prayer is often a lost art that if learned could propel your life to heights unknown. Listening is the intentional act of being still and focusing on what God is saying, has said, or who He's speaking through.

Kenneth Copeland offers four ways to know if you're hearing God. I'm sure there are many other ways, but I believe that these are a great place to start. This would not be something we would emphasize in this resource except that I really believe God values conversation with His children. In fact, A.W. Tozer said, "It's the nature of God to speak." If this is true, then we should have in our nature a desire to listen. Copeland suggest that listening to God requires you to do the following things.

- Check your Receiver
- Find His Frequency
- Learn to Discern His Voice
- Lift Up His Word

I wholeheartedly agree. After hearing Copeland's big four, I thought I would take a moment and simply summarize them in a way that I hope encourages you to add listening to your prayer time.

1. Check Your Receiver

"And you will seek for Me and find Me, when you search for Me with all your heart." –Jeremiah 29:13 (NKJV)

I am not sure if you are familiar with how wireless internet works. In short, you should know that even though it is called wireless internet, there are actually some wires somewhere. It seems wireless to us because there's an invisible signal that connects our mobile device to a router. The router, however, is plugged in and serves as a receiver for the main signal. Somewhere far away is a tower that shoots a communication signal to that router and it connects to your device. If all of that sounds too techy, let me make this really plain. If there was no connection between the tower and the router, you would not be able to communicate. The router is what received the initial signal. If you do not have a router searching for a signal, it will constantly be silent. If you (the router) decide to search for the signal believing that God (the tower) will speak, then listening will have positive results.

Elder Lucretia Mason-Underdue, in her book, *Real Prayer for Real people: Daily Conversation Starters with God* states, "God wants us to communicate with Him because prayer is the connection that brings the relationship between man and God together." This is a reminder that the goal of prayer is not just talking but also listening so that we can come together.

2. Find His Frequency

"They know his voice." –John 10:4 (NKJV)

Recently, I was excited to share in a weekly radio broadcast with my dad. During the COVID-19 season, he began using radio as way to reach worshippers who were socially distanced from the sanctuary. In an effort to get those I knew connected to our radio conversation, I asked him and the producers where our conversation could be heard. His answer was Praise Radio frequency 104.9 FM, 89.1 FM, and AM 1270. I smirked because it honestly had been a while since I had tuned my radio dial to listen to a conversation. However, that was the frequency. Without knowing the frequency, there would be no listening. The key is understanding that the frequency would not change, I just had to make sure to tune into the right frequency.

Similarly, listening to God is knowing that God does not change. He has various methods and a myriad of strategies, yet He is available when you tune into His frequency. Pastor Robert Morris, in his book, *Frequency: Tuning into the Voice of God*, writes that listening allows us to "mature from hearing His voice as sheep to hearing it as His friend to even hearing it as a prophet." There was once a time when you had to work to tune into a program on the radio or television. You had to find the right frequency. You never questioned if it was broadcasting—you knew it was—but you had to do your part to find the frequency and tune in.

3. Learn to Discern His Voice

"My sheep hear my voice." –John 10:27 (KJV)

Have you ever been in a crowd? Maybe you were at an arena or a concert? Maybe you were at a parade and suddenly you heard someone call your name? It's amazing isn't it? With all of the noise that is going on, you somehow manage to hear your name. That is possible not because you know your name, but because you know the voice. Listening happens automatically when you know God's voice. Knowing His voice is something that is created through constant listening. It goes without saying that you do not get to know God's voice if you do all of the talking. No. Listening is how you get used to how God speaks to you, when God speaks to you, and the patterns that God uses when He speaks to you.

Pastor Frank Ntare, author of *Prayers that Overcome Obstacles*, suggests that there is an intimacy developed with God when you listen. In a workshop, he says that in Mathew 7:7 when God says we can ask, seek, and knock, God is really inviting us to get to know Him closer. The ask, seek, and knock is truly an increase in relationship. He models each step in the process with moving from outer court to inner court and finally into the Holy of Holies. In the outer court we ask, at the inner court we seek, but arriving in the Holy of Holies we silent our voices and we knock. May I suggest that when we add listening to our prayer time, we are knocking on a spiritual door that allows God to open up and share a wealth of knowledge, resource, and favor with us.

4. Line It Up with His Word—the Bible

"All Scripture is inspired by God." –2 Timothy 3:16 (NASB)

My son came to me once and said, "Dad, you said you were taking us to get some ice cream." At the time, I was extremely busy and didn't really want to take him. However, he was right. I did say earlier that day that I would take him. So, I am sure you know how this story goes. Yes, you are absolutely right. We went to Sweet Frog for his promised froyo. He did not get that desert simply because he asked. He received it because he reminded me of my own words. He did not allow what was going on around him to decide what he had access to. Listening in prayer is the same.

There are moments after you speak in prayer that you should listen to God's words. Listen to scripture on audio, a sermon, or in silence let your mind recount scripture that you have read before. Listening in this way fills you with his words, so that the next time you pray you can tell God what He already told you. This type of listening requires some perseverance.

Mark Batterson writes a powerful book on prayer entitled, *The Circle Maker*. He contends that "Most of us don't get what we want because we quit praying. We give up too easily. We give up too soon. We quit praying right before the miracle happens." I contend that the miracle he is speaking of can only be expected when you know His word. Listening for God's word and aligning it with His scripture because you listened will bring power to your prayer life.

_____Listening in Prayer

Additional Resources to Help You LISTEN

Here are six books that I have used often in my personal library that have increased my ability and desire to LISTEN TO GOD more often. Each of them are unique and two of them are actual prayers. The books filled with prayers allowed me to read a conversation to God which caused me to listen more and not focus on speaking. I encourage you to consider these, and of course, grow your own library. Reading in and of itself is a form listening. Remember, Romans 10:17 says, "faith comes by hearing."

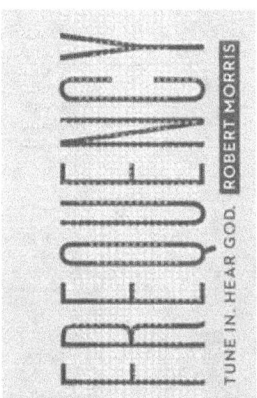  

LEARNING PRAYER
Appendix

> For whatever was written in former days was written for our instruction, that through endurance and through the encouragement of the Scriptures we might have hope.
>
> Romans 15:4

LEARNING PRAYER
Appendix

I. Six Models of Prayer

Please review the six prayer models but note that we are adamant about you learning the ACTS prayer model. While the acronym ACTS itself isn't found in the Bible, we really use it as a core concept for prayer. It can serve as a guide especially when we are learning how to pray. Remember, prayer isn't a formula, and each prayer doesn't have to cover every type of prayer. God wants to hear your heart, feel your emotion, experience your thoughts, know your hurts, and celebrate your achievements. As we grow in our love for Jesus Christ, we will naturally desire to talk to Him more.

These models have been provided for your use from www.salvagedliving.com.

After studying these prayer models, please come back and write which parts of each prayer model you like the most:

_____

_____

_____

_____

_____

_____

Learning Prayer - Appendix

Adoration Confession Thanksgiving Supplication	Honor God with praise Examine your life Ask for help/needs Requests for others Thank God
Praise Repent Ask Yield	Praise Acknowledge Supplication Thanksgiving
Hand: family/friends, teachers, leaders, sick/poor, yourself	Hand: praise God, confess, thanksgiving, intercession, petition

ACTS PRAYER MODEL

Adoration
Confession
Thanksgiving
Supplication

ACTS is the prayer model we recommend that you learn and use the most. When I first learned this method through a Bible study class in college at James Madison University, it became the core for all of teaching on prayer. I first introduced it during a retreat as a 'Wartime Walkie Talkie.' I then noted that the four buttons on the front of the communication device were ACTS, and in order for the walkie talkie to work, you had to flip it over and make sure it had batteries. The battery was FAITH.

Today, I encourage you to commit this model to memory, believe in the God you are praying to, and you will find that as you speaking, God will begin to ACT on your ACTS prayer. Begin by **A**doring and praising God for who He is and the characteristics that make up His being.

Then make a **C**onfession. While this could be difficult, nothing that is easy brings great results or transformation. This is where your prayer will bear the most fruit. I was always taught that if someone does something nice for you, the least you should do is say thank you.

While **T**hanksgiving can be hard when you are in a rough patch and don't feel like God is blessing you, you have so much more to be thankful for than you do to complain about. If there is something more that you think you need, we have a solution for that too.

Go to God in Supplication. This is the moment where you ask God for whatever you desire knowing that He is able to grant you the desires of your heart. Just do not be selfish. Pray asking God to do something for others as well. Bring in others, get outside of yourself and your problems, and carry the burden of those you share life with. *Then* ask for yourself.

This model, as well as the ones to follow, will help get your heart aligned in the proper posture to pray to the Lord. Lastly, do not forget to commit to one of the most underrated aspects of prayer. Commit to the ACT of LISTENING. Just sit, stand, or assume the posture of being still and listen for God's response, instruction, rebuke, or strategy. AMEN.

HEART PRAYER MODEL

Honor God.
Examine your life.
Ask for help.
Request for others.
Thank God.

Start by **H**onoring God with praise. Who is He? What does He do? How do you see or feel Him?

Examine your life, confess the secrets, and the burdens and transgressions you carry. Laying these at the cross will lift a weight you can't even imagine.

Ask for help. Seek help in regard to the confessions you made or just the daily needs in your life. Nothing is too big or too small. God wants it all.

Request for others. One of the biggest blessings we can bestow on another human is prayer.

Thank God. Thank Him for the things He has done, and if your faith is firm, go thank him in advance for the things He will do.

Write your own version of a HEART Prayer:

_____

_____

_____

_____

PRAY PRAYER MODEL

Praise God
Repent
Ask
Yield

The pattern is repeating. This prayer also starts with **P**raising God. Yes, He wants to hear praise, but saying out loud who God is reveals His power in a fresh and encouraging way. It renews and affirms our faith.

Repent. Are you seeing a pattern? God wants us to come to Him with a clean heart. We have to take care of ourselves before we are able to adequately move forward in prayer and relationship. This is often the most overlooked aspect of prayer and it's truly one of the most beneficial portions we can partake in. It's never fun to look in dark corners, and the clean out work is often tough, but friends, please trust me when I say it's so worth it.

Asking is always a great opportunity to let God know how much you trust Him. What you ask for is a statement of your belief in Him.

The last letter stands for **Y**ield, and I really love this word. It means slow down, listen, be still and know (**Psalm 46:10**). Prayer is a two-way conversation, and if we are always talking, never pausing in prayer, we will never hear the sweet truths God has for us. Nor will we hear the answers, forgiveness, and blessings He longs to pour on us. So yield and listen.

Write your own version of a PRAY prayer model:

_____

_____

_____

_____

_____

_____

PAST PRAYER MODEL

Praise for God
Acknowledging the good
Supplication
Thanksgiving

Once again, start with **P**raise for God.

Then move into **A**cknowledging the good He does in your life and the areas you need to confess and reveal. Acknowledging sin is a bold way to say, "I see it, God," and acknowledging is the first step in healing. Oh, how He wants to heal us!

Supplication is once more presenting requests to God on behalf of others and yourself. When you tell someone you will pray for them, do it!

Close with **T**hanksgiving however you feel lead. Thanksgiving for who God is, what He has done, and what He will do. There is no right or wrong "Christianese" lingo you have to use; just talk to God like you would a trusted friend.

Write your own version of a PAST prayer model:

_____

_____

_____

_____

_____

FAMILIAR PEOPLE IN 5-FINGER PRAYER MODEL

If you are a visual person, this prayer model might be an excellent way to walk you through prayer, and they are great for kids or the kid in you.

Starting with your **thumb**, the finger closest to you, begin praying for your *friends and family* – those closest to you!

Your **index finger** represents *teachers* or the outer circle of people that instruct you in any way. These are those who grow you in maturity whenever you are with them, particularly those you communicate with on a regular basis.

The highest finger, your **middle finger**, is for *leaders*. This can include your spiritual leaders, government leaders, local organization leaders, national, and world leaders. There is a lot to be in prayer for on this level!

Your **weakest finger** is a reminder to pray for those that are *sick, weak, poor, and in need*.

The last and littlest **pinky finger** is *you*. You can only care for others when you are at your best. This model is awesome because it keeps the people God has blessed you with right at your fingertips. Since they are there, go ahead pray for them.

Write your own version of a 5 FINGER prayer model:

_____

_____

_____

_____

_____

FAITH IN 5 FINGERS PRAYER MODEL

Another visual way to grow in your prayer life and mature in your faith is to assign faith principles to your prayer.

Starting with your **thumb**, the finger closest to you, begin praying with praise and accolades towards God. Praise opens the door for promise, so give God a thumbs up and start off with praising Him for the things He has done for you.

Your **index finger** represents *confession*. Confession is the guide towards starting over. If unconfessed sins are a weight that hold you down, you will discover that confession and releasing your sins will point you into the right direction.

The highest finger, your **middle finger**, or the one in the center is for you to give thanksgiving to others. God is the one who blesses us, but He often does it through people. Use this finger as a reminder of those that God has partnered you with in each stage of your life. These people stabilize you.

Your **fourth and often considered weakest finger** is a reminder to pray for the weak areas of others. We call this intercession because you stand proxy for someone else. You become strength for them. Use your weakest finger to pray for the weakness of others.

The last and littlest **pinky finger** is for *you*. This finger is small but significant because this is when you lift your own petitions. The old church sung a song that said, "While on others, thou art calling, please do not pass me by." This finger is short, but whatever you ask for in His name, God can show up and do. It is a reminder that our praise, confession, thanksgiving, and intercession are bigger than our own request, but it does not mean that your requests do not matter. God wants to grant you the desires of your heart.

UNPLUGGED

Write your own version of a FAITH 5 FINGER PRAYER model:

_____

_____

_____

_____

_____

_____

II. Types of Prayer

While prayer in its foundational form is simply communicating with God, there are many ways that it can be accomplished in addition to the diverse number of prayer models. The Bible speaks of types of prayer. One of my favorite Bible studying websites (www.gotquestions.org) provides this list as a reference to various types of prayers:

The prayer of faith: James 5:15 says, "And the prayer of faith will save the one who is sick, and the Lord will raise him up." In this context, prayer is offered in faith for someone who is sick, asking God to heal. When we pray, we are to believe in the power and goodness of God (Mark 9:23).

The prayer of agreement (also known as corporate prayer): After Jesus' ascension, the disciples "all joined together constantly in prayer" (Acts 1:14). Later, after Pentecost, the early church "devoted themselves" to prayer (Acts 2:42). Their example encourages us to pray with others.

The prayer of request (or supplication): We are to take our requests to God. Philippians 4:6 teaches, "Do not be anxious about anything, but in everything by prayer and supplication with thanksgiving let your requests be made known to God." Part of winning the spiritual battle is to be "praying at all times in the Spirit, with all prayer and supplication" (Ephesians 6:18).

The prayer of thanksgiving: We see another type of prayer in Philippians 4:6: thanksgiving or thanks to God. "With thanksgiving let your requests be made known to God." Many examples of thanksgiving prayers can be found in the Psalms.

The prayer of worship: The prayer of worship is similar to the prayer of thanksgiving. The difference is that worship focuses on who God is; thanksgiving focuses on what God has done. Church leaders in Antioch prayed in this manner with fasting: "While they were worshiping the Lord and fasting, the Holy Spirit said, 'Set apart for me Barnabas and Saul for the work to which I have called them.' Then after fasting and praying they laid their hands on them and sent them off" (Acts 13:2-3).

The prayer of consecration: Sometimes, prayer is a time of setting ourselves apart to follow God's will. Jesus made such a prayer the night before His crucifixion: "And going a little farther he fell on his face and prayed, saying, 'My Father, if it be possible, let this cup pass from me; nevertheless, not as I will, but as you will'" (Matthew 26:39).

The prayer of intercession: Many times, our prayers include requests for others as we intercede for them. We are told to make intercession "for everyone" in 1 Timothy 2:1. Jesus serves as our example in this area. The whole of John 17 is a prayer of Jesus on behalf of His disciples and all believers.

The prayer of imprecation: Imprecatory prayers are found in the Psalms (e.g., 7, 55, 69). They are used to invoke God's judgment on the wicked and thereby avenge the righteous. The psalmists use this type of appeal to emphasize the holiness of God and the surety of His judgment. Jesus teaches us to pray for blessing on our enemies, not cursing (Matthew 5:44-48).

The Bible also speaks of praying in the Spirit (1 Corinthians 14:14-15) and prayers when we are unable to think of adequate words (Romans 8:26-27). In those times, the Spirit Himself makes intercession for us.

Prayer is conversation with God and should be made without ceasing (1 Thessalonians 5:16-18). As we grow in our love for Jesus Christ, we will naturally desire to talk to Him.

III. Pray in the Name of Jesus

There is a name that causes demons to tremble, sickness to flee, the universe to come into alignment, fear to be silent, and storms to be still. That name is not yours. Nor is it mine. My name is Dwight Shawrod Riddick. I am proudly named after my father, and my son is the third of our family to carry that same name. However, none of our names shake the world. There's another name that does that.

I remember growing up wanting to travel with my classmates on field trips. In order to do so, I had to have permission. Permission was not something my teachers expected my father to come and visit the classroom to speak to her audibly. Instead, she would send me home with a field trip permission slip. The only stipulation was that I had to have my father sign it. It was his name being on the document that granted permission to go places I had never been before.

As I grew older, and had been under the rearing of my father, there came times where I was able to sign my own name. When my wife and I purchased our first home, I signed my name. When I purchased my first car, I signed my name. To be honest, I have acquired many things that I desired signing my own name. However, there are still a few things that are a little more than I can afford alone, where I may have to call on dad and ask for a co-signer. These items are usually huge in value and will take more than one payment to secure. In these cases, I must have my name and someone else's name signed that's has more influence and resources than I do. The co-signer says I have their back on this purchase in case they come up short.

Now, that I am a father, I sent my son out to get things. He often looks at me in awe because the places I send him or things I ask him acquire are well outside of his scope of influence. So, here's what I say to him. Son, when you get there tell them I sent you. Tell them your dad Dwight Shawrod has sent you. It's not at all that I have a great name, but when the person hears that he is connected to me, they understand that he is to be trusted. So, let me be clear: I am not by far JESUS. I am, however, a son. A Son who knows the power of someone else's name. These are simply illustrations that may hopefully help you understand why we pray in the son of God Jesus's name.

Jesus has been blessed by his Father, needed God to co-sign for him, and now vets us before God when we pray.

Let's review again, quickly. First, know that after uttering all those words in prayer, you only are granted permission to obtain those blessings and go further in life with the Permission of Jesus. Secondly, we pray in Jesus's name because He is our co-signer on things we do not have the ability or resources to possess ourselves. Thirdly, He is sitting at the right hand of the Father speaking up on your behalf.

Praying directly to God the Father in the name of Jesus means you recognize and realize that it is only through Jesus and His sacrificial death on the cross that we now have direct access to both Him and His Father in heaven. The Bible is clear in John and in Acts that

> "Jesus said to him, "I am the way, the truth, and the life. No one comes to the Father except through Me." (John 14:6)

> "Nor is there salvation in any other, for there is no other

name under heaven given among men by which we must be saved." (Acts 4:12)

So, when you pray do not forget to say that name. That name gives you permission, grants you more than you deserve, and let's God know that your sins have been paid for, thus making you eligible to have your prayer answered.

IV. Why End Our Prayers With "AMEN"

So, you just spilled your heart out in an emotional and spirit-filled prayer to God. Maybe you were alone or possibly surrounded by a crowd of people. You have used many words and quoted some scripture back to God. You have employed one of the many methods we have spoken of in this book. However, you have to end it. You could just stop praying and start your day. You could not stop praying and not get up, but that would be nearly impossible. So, what do you do to end this prayer? You seal it with kiss and say "AMEN!"

"Amen" is a Hebrew word that means "truly" or "so be it." When we say this at the end of a prayer, we are agreeing with the prayer. We're asking God to please let it be as we have prayed. We are saying we "agree" that all that was spoken is truly possible by our Mighty God.

The Bible uses amen in both the Old and New Testaments. Almost half the occurrences appear in Deuteronomy as God announces punishments for specific sin (Deuteronomy 27:15–26). The people respond by saying "Amen" in agreement with God's justice and in acquiescence to His ways.

The word makes its first appearance in the Bible under the most solemn circumstances. When a husband accused his wife of adultery, and she protested her innocence, and she had not been caught in the act, the matter was settled by God under the test of bitter water (Numbers 5:12-31).

The woman was taken to the priest, and the priest put her under oath. She submitted to a ceremony in which she drank some water containing dust from the tabernacle floor. If she had committed adultery, she was cursed with a wasting disease, but if she did not get sick, then she was proven innocent and her husband was proven wrong.

During the ceremony, when the priest pronounced the curse, the woman was required by God to say, "Amen, Amen" (Numbers 5:22). That is the first occurrence of the word in scripture. The LORD commands it to be said by a person who is yielding herself to examination by Him in his presence

In the Old Testament, amen is linked with praise. For example, in 1 Chronicles 16:36, "… all the people said, 'Amen!' and praised the Lord." Nehemiah 5:13 and 8:6 similarly link saying amen with praising the Lord.

In the New Testament, letters often use amen in connection with praises to God, including letters from John, Jude, Peter, and Paul. Here is one example: "Now to him who is able to do far more abundantly than all that we ask or think, according to the power at work within us, to him be glory in the church and in Christ Jesus throughout all generations, forever and ever. Amen" (Ephesians 3:20–21).

When we pray and end our prayers with amen, we are confessing that what we heard is true, and that God can truly hear and act based on our prayers. Amen is not a magical word nor a plea to conform God to our wills. Rather, it is a statement of confident hope that we make to a God who invites us as His children to come to Him in prayer (Hebrews 4:14–16; 10:19–23; Matthew 7:7–11). We trust that He knows what is best and desire that His will be done (Matthew 6:10; 26:39). When we pray according to God's will, we can be confident that He will grant our requests (John 14:12; 1 John 5:14).

LASTLY, pun intended, amen is how we END our prayers because it has long been used to conclude a moment in the presence of God. If you had not noticed the VERY LAST WORD IN THE CANONIZED BIBLE is, "AMEN" Revelation 22:20-21.

SimplyBible.com notes that the word is almost always used to end a solemn statement, as in the example cited earlier. We find the word amen as the last word in several instances in the Bible.

- The first three books of Psalms end with amen (Psalms 41:13, Psalms 72:19, Psalms 89:52).
- Most books of the New Testament end with it (KJV).
- In the land of Israel, when a prayer or prophecy was made or a law of God was read, "All the people said, 'Amen'" (Nehemiah 5:13, 8:6).
- The Lord's example prayer ends with "Amen" (Matthew 6:13).
- Paul uses the word seven times in his letter to the Romans at the end of doxologies or benedictions (Romans 1:25, Romans 9:5, Romans 11:36, Romans 15:33, Romans 16:20,24,27)
- Paul implies that people should say "Amen" at the end of a prayer in church (1Corinthians 14:16).

The word "Amen" appears therefore to be the fitting last word for solemn utterances made before God. With that being so, I close this entire book with these words.

CLOSING PRAYER BY
DR. DWIGHT S. RIDDICK II

God, you are Lord of all, yet you call us friend. You are almighty in power, unmatched in wisdom, unparalleled in providential strategy, unlimited in your mercy, and creator of all. I admit that our sins often sadden you and attempt to separate us. We all have knowingly and sometimes in ignorance acted against your will. Yet, we know that while you are just in decisions towards us, you are also forgiving.

Thank you, God, for salvation that gives us another chance. While we are aware that the wages of sin is death, you continue to grant us new life. You give us life more abundantly, and for each moment we say hallelujah and glory to your name.

Now God turn our hearts toward you in prayer. Do not allow us to enjoy communicating with others, listening to alternate news, or indulging in filling our ear gates with secular media more than conversing with you in prayer. Ignite a passion in us to escape the world for a moment regularly so that we can grow in intimate relationship with you.

Lord, I am honored by your power to be your servant. I solicit your power to continue serving with Jesus as my example from Hebrews 2:8-10. I ask for your power to serve in leading my family, serving the body of believers that gather at St. Mark Missionary Baptist Church, serving in maturing the disciples of our nation that you have given me Kingdom connections with, serving in sharing the Gospel globally so that all nations and tongues would hear about and get to know Jesus, and serving so that your Kingdom come on earth as it is in heaven.

In the name of Jesus Christ, I, Dwight Shawrod Riddick II, am lifting this petition to you our big brother Jesus, because you alone present us faultless before our Father's throne. This prayer I pray on behalf of my brothers and sisters, on behalf of those you have entrusted to me as spiritual sons and daughters, on behalf of those who live in our community, and most of all to those who are on their way to become believers but have not yet confessed you as the Savior.

I pray this payer in the mathchless, marvelous, and incredible saving name of JESUS CHRIST our Lord, AMEN.

www.ingramcontent.com/pod-product-compliance
Lightning Source LLC
Chambersburg PA
CBHW071023080526
44587CB00015B/2471